Man's inhumanity
to man

Man's inhumanity to man

✦

A close look at race relations in Rhode Island

Nyher Gubloan

iUniverse, Inc.
New York Lincoln Shanghai

Man's inhumanity to man
A close look at race relations in Rhode Island

iUniverse books may be ordered through booksellers or by contacting:

iUniverse
2021 Pine Lake Road, Suite 100
Lincoln, NE 68512
www.iuniverse.com
1-800-Authors (1-800-288-4677)

ISBN-13: 978-0-595-39009-0 (pbk)
ISBN-13: 978-0-595-83400-6 (ebk)
ISBN-10: 0-595-39009-9 (pbk)
ISBN-10: 0-595-83400-0 (ebk)

Printed in the United States of America

Contents

Preface

This is a true story. It is not something from some distance past. You may have seen some of the people mentioned here or had some kind of contact with any of them either by phone or through e-mail as recently as last night before you went to bed. That's not impossible if you really look at the fact that the world is more like one large community.

My pen name is Nyher (N-ì-à) and this is my story. I have no intention to agitate your life or become the conscience of any generation or people. I am not on a mission for anything. I am simply trying to voice my discontent. However, I'm not sure if there is a simple way to write about wickedness of this magnitude without sounding so complacent and condescending at the same time.

I thought I was just a quiet and unknown healthcare professional trying to do my best against all odds until one event turned my world upside down. The racist act of some privileged few in the Attorney General's office got thrown into the hands of some local, so called, investigative reporters interested in glorifying lies and total fabrications. In a jet-like speed, they blew everything out of proportion and I made the evening news followed by a television special all within one week.

Now you have it and this is your chance to read about my experience in an unholy land of absolute profanity. It includes my romantic encounter in search of true love and "the right one." The emotional need and erotic desire of the woman behind it all is fully revealed. And I mean fully revealed. I wish I didn't have to go that deep. Without it, the story is incomplete and there is no way to avoid detailed and explicit account of a relationship that was supposed to be between two consented adults.

In the words of Judith Sills "the path to love is seeded with land mines." What else could be truer! It is interesting to know that some people are still using love as baits to entrap and capture vulnerable, serious minded and dedicated individuals who got side tracked by beauty.

I've been through a lot in life and somehow I knew I would one day write a book about my experience. I knew I would write it out of my desire to help others. But I never thought it would include a 28 days of incarceration as a result of an unholy alliance between a girl friend and some agents of destruction in government and media.

Things could have gone the other way, but I thank God it didn't and I am here instead of being in that big cage known as jail. I'm deeply grateful to many concern friends of goodwill whose demonstration of love and care made it possible for me to be here. I couldn't have been out of jail if I hadn't made the bail and couldn't have made the bail if not for the love of family and friends who cares. To all of those men and women (too many to mention without leaving anybody out), who contributed their hard-earned money to obtain my freedom, I am eternally grateful.

Above all, this book made possible and now goes forward with my deepest gratitude to God almighty for His mercy, love, and care.

1

I thought things were going on well until she started throwing temper tantrums. I'm like what in the world is going on here. It's either you have been hypnotized by some unrealistic expectations or you are simply daydreaming beyond what is humanly possible.

Without saying much with regard to this sudden shift in behavior, she stormed out of the car. The following week was a different Story.

Monday March 9, 1998 started out as just another innocent day with no reason to believe I was about to be betrayed and violated. The sun came out very early. The day looked promising and very comfortable. In a restless and ambitious spirit full of energy, I woke up very early in the morning to prepare for my little girl's 10th birthday in Willow Grove, Pennsylvania. No doubt, I was ready for the four and half hours drive. With some of her gifts packed in my Jeep, I went straight to my office in Providence to attend to the previous request of the Attorney General's office before leaving for PA.

I left my office at about 10:15 am to the Attorney General's office to deliver some client's information they had previously requested. After reviewing the information I brought, I asked Gerard Danna (also known as Gerry) of the attorney general's office to sign that they received those information from me. When I first met Gerard Danna, he introduced himself as an Attorney from the Attorney General's office. He was the primary player and the man behind this type of unspeakable act of man's inhumanity to man. After signing, Gerry asked if it is okay to make a copy of the signature paper. There was no objection. About 30 seconds after he left the room, two middle age white guys walked in, called my name and said, "You are under arrest." Before I could say a word, they started reading the Miranda right.

In puzzled perplexity, I asked myself, what kind of madness is this? Everything bright became blurred. My universe was turned upside down. It felt like blood stopped flowing through my veins, my ears went deaf, and everybody standing looked morose, angry, and mean. For a while I thought I was surrounded by a bunch of hate groups. The only word out of my mouth was "why?" I must have repeated that one word hundreds of times. Within minutes the same television crew from channel 10 who was in my office seven days earlier arrived. Who called them? How long has this been going on? Is this a setup or what?

I was immediately rushed to the courthouse and everything was done so fast. "This can't be true," I kept saying to myself as I stood before the judge. The judge sounded like she was thousands of miles away as she said, "I hereby set your bail in the amount of $150,000 surety bail." I couldn't help thinking about the scale and speed at which this plot was carried out. Just like that, I found myself in the company of other guys in a van going to the Rhode Island Adult Correctional Institute otherwise known as the ACI.

The van pulled up and we (I and others who were arrested on the same day) were all led into the reception area. Needless to say, there's no feeling of happy to be here. If anything, you are surrounded by an aura of this ridiculous feeling of anger and total termination from society.

One of the new guys coming in said, "There is something eerie about this place."
"Tell me about it" was the echoing demand of his stranger partner to whom he was shackled.

Apart from the sound of doors closing or opening here and there; the guard who were trying to control disorderly conduct, or simply making a specific requests; or a bunch of inmates who were just trying to deal with whatever it is as best as they knew how, nothing of interest to arrest your attention.

We were asked to go into one of the rooms on the right, an inmate by the name Mike called out to one of the guards. "Hey Joe! You remember the book I picked up yesterday from the library?"
Joe appeared like as if he wasn't paying attention. Suddenly, Joe yelled back "yeah! What about it?"
"Listen to what it says" Mike yelled back. "Women mature, it is in their glands, their bodies, their life force, but men can experience a host of hells and still they are small boys framed in large bodies."

Without hesitation, Joe roared like an angry Lion "fuck you Mike! You bother me one more time I'm going to make sure you spend the weekend locked up in your cell."

Mike shook his head and murmured to himself "just like the book says, man, just like the book says."

Without warning and nothing to suggest this might happen in a million years, I found myself inside the Intake Service Center of the Rhode Island Department of Correction. Not as a visitor but accused of a crime. No clear understanding of what the charges were. Overtaken by feelings of total hopelessness and despair, I found myself in a muted state of shock. Completely removed from everything I loved, cherished, and depended upon. I'm now alone and powerless, totally cut off. Connection with family and friend severed at least for the moment. I looked around, there were bunch of angry looking, broad chests, dread locks, straight hair, people from different ethnic background, language and creed—in short, a bunch of strange and mean looking guys. Some sad, some happy to be home again, some could care less but most were saying something.

I said to myself "this is it, a place called jail. The only place where time is the enemy. The unholy land of absolute profanity." Trying to feel sorry for yourself or shed tears will do nothing but further demeaning your personality. The best favor you can actually do yourself is to put on a fake macho image. Although I tried it, it didn't quite fall in place.

I guess there was something in my profile or demeanor they all found arrogant and remote to suggest something high and mighty, or mysterious and illusive. Whatever it was prompted about two or three guys to ask "are you a lawyer or…What did you do and why are you here?"

My answer was simply "I have no clue."

Without making a molehill out of a mountain, I decided to blend, yet, remain like a big puzzle. Is not like I have anything to do or going anywhere. I decided to solicit an active role in this unrehearsed life drama, thereby, pay attention to what those around me were saying. I asked the guy sitting next to me; his name is Lawrence Rice who was already explaining something to another inmate about his previous charges. "What did you just say?"

Without remorse, wide eyes with a big smile on his face, he said, "I ate the evidence."

I'm like, "what?"

Adjusting himself a little bit, Lawrence turned slightly and said, "I took the candy bar, unwrapped it, and ate the fucking shit, man. You know what I'm saying? That's the fucking evidence right there. The store wasn't going to press charges but the police nailed me on the violation of my probation. Can you believe that?"

Like someone trying to console himself, he said "you know what! On this new charge, I may get something like ninety days to six months in this joint but I wouldn't know until next week when I appear before the judge."

I asked him "do you have a good lawyer?"

His reply came quickly than anticipated "good lawyer! Are you kidding me? I have no money so I'm hanging on to this bullshit public defender. Hey, this one is simple. On the previous charges, I did not put the wrapper in my pocket that would have constituted shoplifting. I just threw the fucking wrapper across the isle and that's when I got caught."

I tried to see if the two kids on his right side were listening but they were long gone in the resignation with which most now accept their fate.

Needless to say, everybody in this huge cage is here for a reason regardless of whether it was something made up against him or something he actually committed. They are all here young and old, from every race, creed, color, language and culture.

Don't let anybody fool you, none of these, as one of them described it, "sons of bitches" is ready to shed tears or ask for pity—just talk. The one thing they all seem to have in common is the willingness to talk to someone. Besides that, everybody is stone cold to one another's problems.

I decided to listen. There was this frail, a little absentminded, but very gentle elderly Hispanic guy who was doing time for stealing sunglasses. They all like to tease or take a short at him ever since his cellmate announced in the cafeteria that his strong body odor was beginning to make him sick. I asked him about it, his only answer was simply "no English" pronounced 'no inglesh.'

Then came the guy who's tired of his marginalized status suddenly raised his voice and said, "All I ever wanted was a piece of the so called American dream at any fucking prize. Is that too much to ask?" He questioned.

"Calm down." I said to him. "Who do you think I am? A judge?" I asked probingly "What did you do?"

Before he was able to say a word, a guard took him away for some incomplete paperwork. After him was the kid I later nicknamed "magnet." He was, at that time, doing time for grand larceny. Literally speaking, this kid was indeed a magnet for electronic stuff—stereo, camcorder, VCR and "shits like that." He came asking for the meaning of "contradict." You should see the look on his face when I told him what the word "contradict" means. You would think I just parted the Red Sea or knock down the wall of Jericho with my bare hands.

2

At promptly 4:15 p.m., my little girl, Nikisha returned from school in Willow Grove, Pennsylvania. Coming out of the bus, she saw her big sister Becky. With a big smile on her face, she asked, "Is Daddy here?"

"No," Becky said. "He should be here anytime."

Uncertain as to whether Daddy was going to come on time, Nikisha walked towards the front door sluggishly with a disappointed look on her face.

"What's going on Nikisha?" her brother M.J. who was coming out of the house asked.

"She's just a little upset because Daddy who was supposes to be here before 3:30 isn't here yet." Becky responded.

"That's all!" M.J. exclaimed ruefully. "Relax; you're just worrying for nothing. Daddy will be here anytime."

Nikisha went inside. Hours went by and Daddy did not show up. She turned on the television and flipped the channel to Black entertainment and then to MTV. Some of her favorite music videos were playing but nothing was interesting and adequate. The most important thing to her was to see Daddy walk through that door with a big smile on his face. There was no pleasure in anything else. Disappointed and angry, after several hours of waiting and hoping, Nikisha fell asleep on the living room sofa.

◆   ◆   ◆

With a cold chill running through my veins and the wind of uncertainty gently blowing. I said to myself "this is one of those moments I have dreaded all my life." Around 8 p.m., a guard came and ordered all of us to "pick up the basket with your name on it and go to your room."

Ordered! What a strange word. I've always been a free and independent person since the age of maturity. Those freedom and independence are on hold temporarily. I found myself in an environment where you are being told what to do. You eat whatever you are given and they determine how long it should take you to finish your meal. You have no key to your room and no input from you as to how you live your life around here.

The guard determines what time you go to bed and what time you wake up. Forget about your constitutional or fundamental human right. Your play time, otherwise known as rec. (recreation) time and the length of it are determined by people who are not trained to be nice to you but treat you according to a set of rules and regulations.

"Forget about your name." One inmate said. "Around here, everybody is an asshole or motherfucker or son-of-a-bitch." If your cellmate stinks too much and you can't stand it anymore, they would tell you to stop breathing. If you ask, what time is it? You are laughed at. You are becoming demoralized by idleness and nobody gives a damn. All you can do is eat, sleep, and eat and sleep.

How did I end up in this place? I opened my basket. There was a bed sheet, a cover, and a blanket including a small plastic bag that contained one tiny toothpaste and toothbrush, a small bar soap and comb including an extraordinarily small shaving cream. I felt like crying, but it wasn't the right thing to do.

After listening to those stories and problems, my mind shifted to my own. "Loss of income, limited association, public scrutiny and ridicule, feeling of anxiety" within me my family and friends. I began to shiver. How am I going to make surety bail of $150,000? Nobody owes me any obligation to come and see me in jail or get me out. My children are too young to know what to do. I became inundated with fear of having to sit in jail until my case comes up in court in about two months.

I searched my mind but couldn't come up with anything comparable to the scale and breathtaking speed at which those who were active agents of change with regard to my situation carried out their skillful tactics of such unspeakable hatred and destruction.

"Their persistent effort, no doubt seems to be winning at the moment." was my thought. Anticipation of a brighter and rewarding future though occupied my mind was kind of hanging in the balance. But if what the Bible says is true that "the Most High rules in the kingdom of men," then, "this one also shall pass" victoriously was the only hope I had.

Holding on to this hope, I said (thinking out loud) "they will not have my cooperation in their effort to destroy me." I decided to seek God's help through prayer and fasting. I made up my mind to remain without food and without fluid intake including water until justice prevail no matter how long. As a Christian, this is the only choice in the light of my unexpected incarceration.

Marveled by what could have possibly went wrong! I started to wondering and pondering over many things. Some of them were on the fact that I have dealt fairly with every individual I had been fortunate to take care of. I've gone beyond the call of duty to help them. I've never encouraged anyone to do anything illegal either for me or for my company. My mind was all over the place. Not knowing what the charges against me were did not make things any easier.

In a note I left next to my bed I wrote, "All my life I've been struggling. I am tired of having to deal with the demonic acts and tactics of people of evil intent. As much as I love life, I wouldn't like to cooperate with evil. If this is the end of my journey, I would like to accept it courageously." I ended the note with "I remain as always, in God's hands." This was just a note that came out of my bewilderment and not necessarily a suicide note.

The word got out and I was immediately placed under suicide watch. Reverend Yany, a very pleasant man with genuine kindness came. To some inmates, he is known as "that short dude with the Church thing around his neck." When we met, Reverend Yany introduced himself as a fellow African from Cairo in Egypt the birthplace of his mother. His father was born in Greece. Perhaps he is an American by birth or naturalization, you couldn't tell. Nothing to suggest he wasn't born in this country.

We sat down in a very small office room across from the guards' station. We sat facing each other. He reached out, held my hands and asked, "Shall we pray?"
I nodded.
After the prayer, Reverend Yany asked, "How can I help you?"
Tears welled up in my eyes; I looked the Reverend straight in the eyes and demanded "why am I here? What did I do wrong?"
There was no answer from the Reverend just a nod.
"All my life I've been struggling and never turned my back on those who needed my help along the way. And this is what you get for being nice and law abiding?"

"Remember Jesus—arrested, tried and convicted, crucified and died on the cross all for no fault of his own." The Reverend winced.

"That was for righteous cause, but…Even though I am a Christian but…this is me in here as a business man" was the thought going through my mind. Like someone seeking self-justification, I said to the Reverend "I've bent backward and gone beyond the call of duty to help my clients and everybody I've come across." Then asked, "Does anybody care about what I have done right?"

The Reverend shrugged and said "but God cares." Clearing his throat, he continues, "in here are people who are seriously bad and those who are here for no fault of their own. They are all children of God and are equally precious in God's eyes." Finally, the Reverend made a promise to bring me the Bible and also help get in touch with my friends and loved ones I've been unable to reach because of the fact that their phones will not accept collect calls.

Going back to my cell, I heard my number announced over the intercom. "I—4 bottom, visitors! I—4 bottom, visitors!"

I asked one of the guards "where do I go?"

He looked so surprised "visiting room, where else?"

"I know that. Where is the visiting room?"

"Go down to the 1st floor and turn left" he said as he shook his head.

Waiting there patiently and perhaps wondering was Reverend V.O. a friend and a brother in Christ. He looked surprised at seeing me in an inmate uniform. As I was about to sit directly across from him, he asked while still holding on to that surprise look on his face "what happened? I saw the television special on channel 10 and I was shocked."

My response was somewhat similar to the one I gave Reverend Yany.

Brother V.O. held my hands and said, "let us pray." After a short prayer, he promised to contact other friends so they can all work together for my release. Before saying good-bye, he reminded me "there are so many people out there waiting to see you including Reverend P.F. and his wife."

About two seconds after he left the visiting room, Reverend P.F. and his wife walked in. Numbed and also shocked at seeing me in the inmate uniform, they both stood motionless. With mouth held agape in disbelief, his wife shook my hand and in a shallow breath, gently whispered "we are praying for you."

Reverend P.F. and I have known each other since 1973 when we first met as members and co-revivalists. We lived together for so many years and really have a lot in common. We became such a good friend and remained so against all odds. The binding tie is more than just friendship; it's the blood of Christ. Slowly in comforting voice slightly above whisper, he repeated what his wife said earlier "we are praying for you and I want you to know that the devil is a liar."

Relief eased into my smile. It's always good to know that somebody cares.

"Our main concern is to get you out on bail so you can have time to prepare for this case and that also is the concern of your wife and children."

Quizzically, I asked "my what?"

"Your wife," then paused "she's been crying and worried sick, calling everybody since the news reached her. She's the one organizing and trying to raise the bail money." Looking straight into my eyes he said, "Please, call her tonight."

"What am I suppose to say? Thank you?" I snapped.

"That's not what we are asking you to do." His wife said sharply. "Call her and please do it for Christ's sake."

After divorce, times have neither erased nor healed whatever set us against each other. Forgive, no doubt, but forget? I wish I could. It's very difficult to forget. Maybe I would someday see the past as a teacher not an enemy and that might help dispel the sour taste of it all. Who knows? For now, the hurt and pain of the past are much too real and too early to forget.

"Perhaps the magical property of time will eventually do the healing." Mrs. P.F. said with a warm smile. "All we are asking you to do right now is leave it in God's hands." With a sympathetic squeeze in her voice, she went on "your angry words now and then are as meaningless as her past insulting and offensive words and deeds. Let go, my brother, and let God."

Coming back to my mod (cell), a fellow inmate yelled out "I understand you went there to talk to Reverend Yany today, could you ask him if I can have a Bible?"

"What do you need a Bible for?" His cellmate asked. "You think God is interested in you? You better get your act together before God sets you on fire or strike you with lightening."

Tired and marooned in my own worries, as I was about to say something, another inmate tapped me on the shoulder. "Stay away from that asshole. What does he think God is going to do for him?" With a shift in his voice, he went on

"I'm telling you that shit head is bad news, man. Forget it, he is beyond redemption."

"I don't know of anyone who has lived my life around here." A voice from behind me said softly. It was that of Steve Antonelli who described himself as a full blooded Italian. "I had a good job, a house, a car and money in the Bank." He was a former marine with honorable discharge. "For 14 years I worked for the Rhode Island Department of Economic Development." He said with a slightly mean smile, the tone of his voice rose sharply. "In 1984, I went for spinal surgery and the medication the Doctor gave me screwed up my system. I developed addiction as a result of heavy-duty narcotic. The pain didn't go away but increased over time." Drawing out the word in an annoyed fashion, he went on. "I lost my wife, family disowned and disregarded me. Friends were methodically severed from my life. I ended up in jail, and then came out only to discover there was nothing left and I mean nothing not even underwear." With a shallow breath, he giggled, "Just when I thought I had reached the apex of my problems," he shrugged. "I was hit with Gillian Barrel syndrome. I became completely paralyzed and the pain escalated more than ever before. Do you know what Gillian Barrel syndrome means?' He asked with a quizzical look on his face.
    I nodded.

John Campaniello, a friend of Steve, shook his head and said, "This fucking state is a country on its own with its so many bullshit laws designed to make criminals out of descent people."

Steve sighed, and then nodded "now I'm here for passing heroine and for shoplifting. I'm telling you, the addiction is really doing a number on me and nobody seems to care." The annoyance and frustration were edging his voice. "There was a time I asked the judge to send me to jail because I didn't have anywhere to go. I've checked myself into the psychiatric ward just to have a warm place to stay because it was cold outside. I'm here now till November and...I...don't know where my daughter is, my only daughter, a 16 years old little girl. I used to reach her at this number," he tossed a paper forward, quivering and very angry. "The fucking number doesn't take collect calls anymore and I have no way of knowing where she's at and if she's all right. I may not get out of this place until November and I don't know where I'm going to go."

3

The following morning was another ordinary Thursday later turned the most miserable day of my life. As the sunlight began to burn the fog and the night's mist, a Correctional Officer by the name Dan Daquila came over the intercom to announce to everybody in the mod "get up, make your bed and get ready for your morning recreation time you fucking assholes." He hammered it in with such a loud laughter "ha ha ha......ha," then went on "if you forget to make your bed, you will be locked up in your cell for two days you bunch of babies" followed by more laughter "ha ha ha......ha."

It was 7:45 in the morning and the Today Show was running a story on President Bill Clinton and the unfortunate problem he found himself. Katie Couric displaying her familiar trademark smiles as she said, "this is Today on NBC." After that, they ran about two commercials and there it was—my picture along with others as Channel 10 announced that they have a special on Home Health care coming on tonight at 7:00 p.m.

In a colorless tone of voice, I asked one of the inmates "when is our last recreation time today?"
"Why are you asking?" he asked
"Because my story is coming up at 7 p.m. on Channel 10." I responded with a shallow breath.
"Your what?"
"My story."
"Well, our last recreation time ends at 6:45 p.m. tonight."
Without wasting time, I asked some of the inmates whose recreation time is coming up after ours to "kindly watch Channel 10 at 7 p.m. may be I would have an idea why I'm here."
They all agreed to.

The following morning, C.O. Daquila's usual announcement with his sarcastic loud laughter woke me up. Bed made with no place to go not even the cafeteria. As I was brushing my teeth, an inmate from about two cells to my right came knocking "hey Doc.! Bad news. That's one big fucking bad news, man."

"What did they say?" I asked curiously.

"Why don't you come with me to the cafeteria, give me your breakfast in exchange for the full story." He said with a big smile on his face.

"Sure, why not!" I wearily shook my head.

Slowly but steadily he started given me the story, which according to him ran for about 15 minutes on television. "Those accusations seemed bogus and unreal to me." He said. "And those two women looked like they were nothing but liars and junkies" was his judgment. "I couldn't believe that those cruel and wounding words were said about you on a statewide television for thousands if not millions of people to see."

He looked at me peeringly from the corner of his eyes while drawing a spoon full of cold cereal and quizzically beginning to repeat the accusations again. He shook his head as he screamed, "this state is all fucked up, man." One by one, he gave me all that he was able to remember.

Those words stung deeply and hurt so badly. Shaking, sweating, and completely out of breath I whispered to myself "God, why did you allow this to happen to me?" Full of emotionally charged resentment, I wished some kind of higher power could lift me out of the cafeteria only to reappear in my cell without speaking a word to any man.

I felt a hand on my right shoulder. I turned; it was the guy sitting next to me on the right. Drinking his milk he said "you see that guy over there? That black dude with short dreadlocks? He is a lawyer. Talk to him."

Before I could say a word, he called out "hey Ronnie, when you have the chance talk to the Doctor."

Ronnie nodded, then said sharply "Doc., don't worry about it I saw the story. Those girls are liars. No intelligent person would believe those things they put together against you." He smiled angrily and shook his head. "They always like to destroy sincere, intelligent and law abiding people who want to earn their rightful place in the society through hard work." Pointing at me, he said "you are going to need a good lawyer if you don't want these people to really screw you up. Why don't you find time so we can meet at the Law Library? I would like to show you some stuff you can share with your lawyer..."

Just as Ronnie was about to finish his last sentence, another inmate by the name Joseph Vasquez called out "hey Doc.! I understand you are going to be doing a story about your experience in this shithole!"
"Yeah, maybe." I said

With a big lump on his throat, angry and unable to smile, he said, "I'm doing time for being a Public Nuisance. Can you believe that?" He inquired. "What is that anyway? I'm not supposed to go out anymore? I went to visit a friend and I ended up here."
I asked him "were you aware your friend was doing something illegal?"

Without answering my question, he stared angrily at the cold meal in front of him as he raised the tiny cup of cool aid given to him. His jaw clenched like someone fighting back tears. "Now I'm being served with this crap!"
I couldn't help but noticing the pained expression on his small face as I asked him "how old are you son?"
Without hesitation, he said, "I just turned 18 about a month ago."

As a father, I was overcome by emotion, something I was not prepared to show regardless. The few days I've been here was nothing but days of wondering and total confusion. First of all, I have no clear understanding as to the reason for my arrest. Second of all, they refused to give me a copy of the complaints against me. Thirdly, everybody seems to be interested in talking to me about his or her problems and there is nobody I could talk to about mine but God. Is this by some kind of divine design or a call of destiny for me to become the listening ears to the problems of these guys?

Trying to lighten the mood, an elderly African American man sitting across from me said with a warm and inviting smile "Did you see how fast the food you gave to that guy disappeared? God forbid the government should forget to do groceries shopping around here, this bunch will shred this place."
I smiled.
"Its good to see you smile, son." He said gently. "Don't forget, the sun will rise again."
I haven't seen that elderly man since then.

◆   ◆   ◆

Ronald Chase, otherwise known as "Ronnie." born in Philadelphia in 1950. His mom a very religious woman was a member of the Narragansett Indian Tribe and his father was born in Philadelphia. Ronnie, a very intelligent individual graduated from Sayers Junior High in Philadelphia but never went to high school. Got caught up in the black power struggle during his teenage years.

Ronnie, with his calm and always smiling face, looks younger than his age. As a child growing up, he became so irritated by what he described as "the unfortunate demeaning plight of my brothers and sisters." He became angry by the huge number of the poor, the hungry, and the homeless within the Black community in the '60s, Ronnie, a member of Islamic faith, decided to join the Black Panthers. Haven't read "The Destruction of Black Civilization" by Chancellor Williams, and also about famine and starvation, and how people were dying slow death in Africa, South America and the West Indies while the Europeans and those in the United States of America are enjoying abundant wealth. How they were advancing in technological know how slowly but steadily and "my people wandering in abject poverty." Ronnie decided to take the militant approach.

In 1971 he was arrested for possession of machine guns, hand grenade, dynamite etc. Needless to say, this put him on the FBI, CIA, and the whole gamut of government watchful eyes' list. He was branded "public enemy." Because of his effort to help himself, Ronnie developed interest in Law Education. He is now a self taught paralegal hoping that some day he would realized his dream of becoming a lawyer. So far, he had successfully defended himself on several occasions and won.

I asked him concerning his current charges.

"I'm in jail for assault on a girl who's neither a girl friend nor an acquaintance but one you might describe as a hooker." He grinned. "We met in a drug rehabilitation program and the girl developed interest in me in exchange for some drugs promised to her by an individual responsible for my arrest." He tried to reach back into his mind for the detail, but it was lost in a quietly displayed angry outburst.

With a warm smile, trying to divert his attention from the grim reality of the awful reminder of the past, I asked, "how can you be of help to me? My lawyer is on vacation till next week."

He chuckled and said, "I might be able to show you what materials you may need to prepare for your case." Reaching into his buried memories, he said, "I remember a case similar to yours." With a shift in his voice, he went on "I tell you what, why don't you meet me at the Law Library tomorrow afternoon."

"Sure." I responded. However, when I approached the guard in charge of our mod for permission to meet with Ronnie at the Law Library the following day, the answer was a resounding "no."

When he heard about the reaction to my request, Ronnie snapped. His voice flat and cold as he said "may be it's time for a change. I've been living in a perpetual charade with no special regard for wealth and denied myself the good things of life." He shook his head.

"I couldn't have said it better" was my response. "You cannot effectively help the poor by remaining poor yourself." I said sharply. "You are a man of special passion and if you don't mind my being blunt, I think the passion is misplaced, thereby, lost sense of direction long before now."
"You think something is wrong with me?" He asked.
"I am a Christian not a judge." I said.
"I want you to be honest." He demanded.
"You are a man who understands the Law. What you need is expungement, not of record, but of your mind."
Surprised by my honest evaluation of him, he wheezed. "How do you mean?"

Looking at him straight in the eyes, I said, "no matter how angry we get or how hard we try, we will not completely understand philosophically, theologically or otherwise the reason for the existence of sin and evil in this world. Some people have dedicated their lives to making sure that hate and prejudice does not go away. Trying to please them or make peace with them will not affect what is deeply ingrained in them. They are on a mission to destroy lives and they will do it without remorse and without the fear of God."

He nodded as he sat motionless and very attentive.

"The Bible says 'vengeance is mine, says the Lord, I will avenge.'" I continued.

I said, "Ronnie, you need to operate from the position of strength. Get out of this place, go back to school and get your law degree and you will discover how effectively you are able to help not only our people but all of God's children."

With a big smile on his face, he said, "you are right, you are absolutely right."

He had barely finished when an elderly white individual of about 80 years old by the name Gene Demmler walked up to me and said, "I better follow you, you seems to know where we are going."

"We are going to the Cafeteria." I said

"I'm new here. I don't know anywhere." He said.

"What are you here for?" I asked.

"Five parking tickets." He had a surprise look on his face.

"Parking tickets?"

"Yes! I wonder how much is costing the government to keep me locked up!"

"That's an interesting way to look at it. Can't they just ask you to pay the money and get out?"

"I paid the tickets, but, according to them there is a new law and part of the requirements of the law is that with five tickets or more, you get thrown in jail for 30 days, or do community service or house arrest for 20 days.

The words of John Campaniello quickly came to mind "Rhode Island is its own country."

"What do you do for living?" I asked Gene.

"I'm a CEO of a small manufacturing company known as M & M Tools with offices in Florida and Rhode Island." He responded. Confused and unable to see clearly because (according to him) his glasses were taken when they booked him, he looked at the wall clock and said, "I may get out before 5 p.m." It was about 10 minutes before 5 p.m.

◆　　　◆　　　◆

I was overtaken by a morbid chill at the sound of the word "nigger" coming from Blacks to Blacks. Shock held me motionless with gnarled knuckles. I looked at the faces of these men, how they were so happy to call each other "niggers" like as if there's nothing to it. Every sentence punctuated with this grotesque, disgusting, despicable, distasteful, and one of the most forbidden words ever invented in the history of mankind. This word is to every Black man and woman anywhere in the world a reminder of the ugly past—a legacy of the inexpressible cruelty of slavery, segregation, and racism. One of the most provoking instruments of any hate group past and present. "Nigger" is the most dangerous, insidious, and ugly word in the history of English language.

A lot of people of incredible talent, passion for the human family, extraordinary intelligence and boldness have lost their freedom and ultimately their lives in their effort to defeat bigotry. No single word in history has ever affected lives negatively. Many careers ruined, emotional and physical scars suffered by many.

The word "nigger" epitomizes the worst act of man's inhumanity to man. It represents a haunting, poignant and powerful sword capable of doing damage beyond human imagination. This heart piercing and shattering word invented and nurtured by the vitriolic act of the racist few is now been sustained and glorified in a special way? To find it rolling so freely and loosely on the lips of those who are not even suppose to remember it anymore is more than shocking.

This "don't-ever-call-me-that-anywhere" but "it's-okay-for-me-to-call-myself-that-even-in-your-presence" attitude is no doubt equal to "do-as-I say but don't-do-as-I-do" unwritten rule of bad behavior. I don't think there is anything either in any constitution or the natural law to justify this kind of self-inflicting wound even if no pain is felt. When a white person calls you "nigger," you know the reaction will no doubt be swift, severe, and ugly. Why then are we doing it to ourselves? "God is no respecter of persons." Neither is the law. There is no credible explanation to justify why I should hurt myself and society cheers.

4

Three weeks after my arrest, still in jail and unable to make the bail, my Lawyer brought me a copy of the complaints. He told me that the court just gave it to him and couldn't understand why the attorney general's office refused to make it available right from day one.

The complaints revealed six counts of indictment so baseless, unreal, and untrue. The fact that they were nothing but a complete fabrication of lies and rumors made me question the integrity, sense of reasoning and intelligence of the person responsible for my arrest and the writing of the complaints. With a little more time on the examination of records to determine the fact, he could have discovered the truth without being told what the truths are.

There were five major players in this ridiculous scheme of unspeakable cruelty: Eileen Figuerado, my Office Manager; Dan Walsh, a Social Worker at the Newport office of the Department of Human Services; Brenda Carney, a client; Tracey Camara, a homemaker; and Cheryl Arruda, my girl friend who took over when Eileen left as the office manager.

According to the Affidavit signed by Gerard Danna of the RI Attorney General's office, "This investigation was commenced as a result of a phone call that I had received from Dan Walsh, a Social Worker for the Department of Human Services Newport office on November 14, 1997." Information revealed by Gerry Is on page 48–49. Dan made the so called allegations regarding our billing practices (according to Gerard Danna). The entire affidavit was so disconnected and unreal it defies logic. However, upon receiving this phone call from Dan, Gerard Danna went to the home of Eileen. He did not come to my office to verify Dan's allegations. Eileen left my company a few days after the allegations were made and she left on the advice of Dan Walsh.

Eileen, slightly privileged, became my office manager on the recommendation of my company's Nursing Supervisor—Doreen Cabral who's known Eileen for so many years. She said a lot of good things about Eileen but either intentionally or unintentionally left the most important piece of information out.

Eileen, a very computer literate individual was also eager to learn. She's no stranger to HTML and website development. Masked by brilliant imagination, unfettered perfection and efficiency, she won my trust. In-spite of her long commute from Pawtucket to Middletown, she was always in on time. The brightness in her eyes and actions gave me confidence and no reason to doubt or be suspicious of her. Her splendid smoothness when it comes to dealing with social workers and case managers from various sources of client referrals was just what I had been looking for. I was loath to believe everything I've seen about her without the slightest reason to doubt. Her loyalty and dedication looked so real with nothing to suggest anything diabolical.

When Bob Lake of the Electronic Data Services (EDS) came to my office to explain how to submit Medicaid billings, without hesitation, I asked him to go ahead and train my office manager—Eileen Figuerado. Bob took his time and carefully explained everything to Eileen. She became my confidant. I must have repeated the importance of billing for the exact hours of services rendered hundreds if not thousands of times. There was a time she crossed out something on the cover page of her first billing papers about to be sent to the Department of Human Services. I caught that before mailing it and said to her "I don't like crossing things out like that."

She asked, "Are you going to make me rewrite this cover page because I crossed something and rewrite the correct number next to it?" She shook her head in disbelieve.

I showed her how to find the exact hours "you have to wait until we have all employees' time slips, and then take the hours directly from each time slip signed by clients and plug that into billings. Because a client is authorized 10 hours a week does not mean we have to bill for 10 hours if we are not there for the entire 10 hours. We bill for exact hours of services rendered—if we are there for only 6 hours, that's what we are going to bill for and not the 10 hours authorized."

The fact that she followed this simple instructions initially for about two or three billing periods gave me enough confidence to trust that she would always do it right. Besides being preoccupied, every once in a while, with some disturbing question, thought or feeling, and occasionally react irrationally, there was nothing alarming. Although there was a time I caught her looking at me, and then shifted as if it might reveal a too private secret. She once had a very severe angry outburst with Doreen on some private matters. It was resolved very quickly.

She was extraordinarily ambitious and extremely eager to know everything about home health care as quickly as possible. At first, I was leery thinking that she might gain this knowledge and take off on me. So I said to her "Eileen, you have to remember that 'Rome was not built in a day.' Let's take things one step at a time."

Within a few weeks Eileen was calling Dan "dan dan." There was a time Dan apologetically said to Eileen "if it seems like I'm coming on to you please let me know, I don't mean to." Eileen quickly brushed it aside and said to him "don't be ridiculous, Dan. I know you are simply kidding with me that is why I calls you 'dan dan.'"

Few days after, things changed. Gradually and systematically the jokes were becoming a reality. Eileen developed a crutch. Dan invited Eileen to his office and from there; a lunch date arrangement was made. Eileen discussed this with some of our clients and an employee by the name Denise MaClin. According to Denise, Eileen later revealed it to her psychiatrist.

One morning in August of 1997, Eileen's sister Coleen Bamford came with Eileen to meet with the insurance representative to discuss full medical coverage that would include Eileen's entire family. Our Middletown office was just a one large room office. Coleen sat directly facing my desk. Her perpetually pleasant face held my attention as I smilingly inquired of her without living my desk "your sister told me you are a social worker, is that right?"

She's a woman of few words. She said "yes" and immediately retreated into a shy and remote silence.

On my way to the conference room, I made a passive comment to Eileen who was coming from the same direction "your sister is very nice and a pleasant woman."

Beaming with a smile at my comment, she asked "you like my sister?"

"Who wouldn't?" was my innocent response as I walked away.

Eileen later discussed this with her sister and gave her my E-mail address and from there an affair developed. We went out for about three weeks. Her first weekend at my place was according to her remarkable. When she came on Friday night, she told me she'd be back at her place the following afternoon but did not leave until late Sunday night. She had this teenage-like euphoria she hadn't felt, as she later declared, in years. It no doubt gave her a delicious sense of belonging. Gradually but steadily, within days, she was beginning to nurture such a strange and irrational notion of nothing matters but the two of us.

Couple of weeks later, I went to Philadelphia very early on Saturday morning to see my children. I didn't come back until Sunday night. When I came back, it was too late to call her; besides, I was too tired and exhausted.

The following morning, Eileen was the first person to get to the office. Again, she looked preoccupied and tense like a wary cat surveying hostile surroundings. Her eyes red with rage as she took out a small plastic bottle of medication, opened and took some, then quickly closed the plastic bottle and secretly returned it in her packable. About ten minutes later, her mood started to reverse, and then made a casual comment "I think I'm going crazy."

I couldn't say anything assuredly. Looking straight into her eyes, I asked in a voice full of insistent passion "are you in therapy for something I should know as your employer?" The seriousness of the look on my face, my mood and demeanor were bent on knowing the truth.

Her eyes widened and her face portrayed a picture of displeasure, yet, she did not speak a word.

I took a deep breath, the words agonizing to say as I asked, "who is your therapist or shall I say your Psychiatrist?"

With tear-filled eyes, she said, "I think something is wrong with me." After that there was uncomfortable silence for several moments, and then the phone rang. We left the office at 5 p.m. exactly and did not go any further with that discussion.

At my house around 7:30 p.m., Entertainment Tonight just started and Mary Heart was saying something when my phone rang. It was Coleen. "Why didn't you call me over the weekend? Why didn't you call me today?" She yelled.

"I…I didn't come back from Philly until late Sunday night. Tired and exhausted, I…" Before I could finish the last sentence, she hung up.

I quickly called back. Trying to let her know that her reaction was unfair and rude. In a loud, frustrated and irrational voice, she yelled, "Are you going to marry me. I would like to know right now. Are you going to marry me? I wouldn't like to waste my time if that is not what you intend to do."

"First of all, this is not the right time or the right place to make such a serious commitment. Second of all, I think you guys have some serious emotional problems that needs to be taken care of right away." I said in an angry tone of voice. "Your action tonight is uncalled for. And when I compared that with what happened to your sister at the office today, I'm afraid, my answer to your proposal is no." I snapped.

She stopped coming around and our relationship ended shortly thereafter.

5

I needed to hire more employees. Ads were placed in some local newspapers. Responses to our help wanted ad in the Fall River newspaper were very impressive. First week alone I interviewed more than 20 people at my Fall River office who were interested in working as home health aide.

Three weeks later, just as I was coming from lunch, they gave me a completed application and the girl at the front desk was telling me that the applicant just left. I went in my office, waited for about 20 minutes, and then, called the number on the application. "May I speak with Cheryl please?"

"Speaking." The voice on the other end said softly.

"I got your application. Would you like to come for an interview this afternoon?"

"I'll be right over." She said.

About 45 minutes later, Cheryl walked in. I then called her into my office. Whether by accident or design, I found myself paying attention to her. The fact that she was a whole lot younger than her age was too real to ignore. Her sparkling eyes, her voice so sexy and seductive it was like a magic spell and I couldn't withdraw myself. Just like that, I promised to hire her for office job in about a month if she would improve her typing skill. I even offered her the chance to come and practice at my office in the afternoon if she wouldn't mind.

Cheryl came not with any kind of special academic achievement or innate gifts. Besides the fact that she's been in health care for so many years as a home health aide, she had nothing special or marketable skill. Her typing was too slow for any busy office and had no computer knowledge. Her knowledge of office work was in fact below average. With a recurring peptic ulcer, intermittent back pain and low blood, she came looking for job. Covered with outstanding beauty and irresistible body and smile, she found her way to my office.

Was it by mere coincidence or perverted fate that brought the two of us together? It didn't matter. About two afternoons later, Cheryl made an unrelated comment during one of our discussions that sets my mind raging like inferno. I was explaining some wonderful and interesting stuff she could do or accomplish using Microsoft Office. She looked at me and said "I bet you like your computer more than you like sex."

That prompted a whole lot of questions and discussions, which led to the promise of a date. Without hesitation, I asked, "Would you like to go out with me?"

Looking away from me, Cheryl said in low but emphatically tone of voice "yes." She then turned confidently as she repeated herself with a nod "yes I will go out with you," She leaned forward across the desk and gave me a quick kiss.

The following day, she brought some gifts for me. The first was a song "Power of Love" by Laura Branigan on CD and the same song by Celine Dion on cassette tape. The second gift was some nude erotic pictures of her taken, according to her, by her husband before their separation. She pulled out one of the pictures—a close-up taken in a sitting position. In the picture, she was wide opened before the camera. With her index finger on the private part, she said "it's all yours now."
"Really!" I exclaimed.
"You heard me!" She responded.

Although Cheryl is somewhat more like an introvert but never afraid to express her love anywhere and at any time regardless of who may be watching. She like to hold hands, kiss when necessary, and hug anywhere. Her manners although short of being exquisite but always lady-like.

The following Saturday, we agreed to go to the movies. After a brief time at the mall where she picked up some necessary items, we went straight to my place in preparation for our date. As soon as we walked in, she asked "where is the bathroom?'
"The room on your right." I said

After using the bathroom, she went into the bedroom, which was directly across from the bathroom while I was in the kitchen looking for something to drink. She saw the Celine Dion tape she gave me a few days earlier on my bedroom stereo and decided to play it.

There were so many good and interesting movies to choose from. But when I entered the bedroom, seeing her shining, long and fluffy blonde hair covered the pillow and her petite body glowing and beckoning with that Princess Diane's shy look on her face as she lied in bed. The "Power of Love" by Celine Dion gently playing. I said to myself, to heck with the "Titanic" I'm staying on this ship. The "Soul Food" couldn't be better. And believe me, for one day any rightful thinking person would rather be the "Nutty Professor" in this "As Good As It Gets" action pack which was about to begin.

I became almost like the "Flubber." You know, the invention of the absent-minded professor—lying in bed next to her with my shoes on, then get up to kick off my shoes, while making sure she's comfortable. I was loosing my mind and I could care less.

It's been such a long time since I felt like this. The first time was when I was still dating my X-wife. It was on a bright Saturday afternoon. She called and asked me to come over. When I got to her place we both lost control and with one illuminating look and a smile the situation was difficult to resist. In a jet-like speed, the mutual reaction that followed took the two of us beyond the twilight zone. Shortly thereafter, I proposed to her.

Now I'm single. Haunted by the demons of loneliness and need, my body's crying for genuine love and affection or maybe just a lustful desire, I couldn't think straight. At first, I felt somehow uneasy at touching Cheryl. But that mysterious and inviting smile and the dimples in her cheek deep as dark chasms molded me into believing that "yeah, this one is mine."

When my hand touched her hands, skillfully caressing her body, I reached out to her breast, her stomach and her thighs. She did not fight the arousal but simply allowed it to take her fears and worries to a new height of sensation and lust while teasing the rigid peaks until she moaned with desire. The moaning was rising steadily as I became highly delighted in the feel of her.

When it was over, I looked at her face. Her smile warmed and brightened. Caressing as she rub her cheek on my chest and giggling when her hands touched between my thighs. Her wide eyes filled with delight as she breath softly and said, "You are a very strong man." Emphasizing the word "strong," slowly and gently, she rose up and was on top of me. We went on again and again for maybe four or five times within a period of about 6 hours.

I brought Cheryl back to her house around 7:45 p.m. That night, she called me three times before 4 a.m. During our last conversation, around 3:45 Am., she said "I can barely wait to be in your arms again."

At seeing Cheryl in Fall River the following Monday, Eileen became extremely angry. The rumbling of resentment and…Agitated and infuriated, she snapped. "She's your girl friend. Isn't she?" She asked with a reproach look.
"Of course, yes."
"You left my sister for this bimbo!"
"Don't say that—please."

The following day Eileen came to the Middletown office sobered and very apologetic. "I was out of place yesterday. I'm really sorry for yelling at you like that." She said.

"I'm beginning to be concerned about your combative attitude and occasional mood swing. I don't know how long you've been trying to hide this! Perhaps you think you can deal with it. You really need to seek help."

Like someone trying to avoid a blistering lecture, she said, "I know. I've been seeing a psychiatrist lately and I was just going to ask you for permission to have every Monday off. Monday is the day I go to see this Psychiatrist and believe me this is something I'm quite sure I have to deal with."

Holding her hand, I said passionately "you are a very intelligent woman, and very caring too. You need to deal with whatever it is and don't let it eat you up and destroy you."
This gave her confidence enough to open up to me but couldn't get over the fact that Cheryl had taken her sister's place. Initially, the two of them couldn't get along. When Cheryl came to the Middletown office for the first time, she did not look at Eileen eye to eye and neither did Eileen. But days went by and they gradually eased into talking to each other directly and laughing at each other's jokes.

Shortly after that, Eileen started to include Cheryl in everything and she slowly earned Cheryl's friendship and trust. They quickly followed it all up by exchanging gifts and phone calls.

"Does he know about this?" was the question Eileen asked as I walked in on one of their telephone conversations. She looked at me and chuckled.

I knew right away she was talking about me. I asked curiously "who's that?"

"It's your girl friend—Cheryl." She responded with mouth away from the phone as she whispered, "she thinks she's pregnant."

When the conversation was over, I warned her to stay away from Cheryl because of the fact that Cheryl is too trusting and she knew I loved Cheryl greatly.

Somehow, there was something in this unholy union that made me thought of Eileen for the first time as a diabolical and conniving individual whose mind was bent on something.

6

It was around noontime on a cloudy and depressing day. Like someone trying to find an outlet for frustration and inner conflict, Cheryl asked with a pleading look "could you take me to your place? I'm too tired and I need to just relax and rest."

"Sure." I responded.

The rental car I brought to the office did not have any open space between the driver and the passenger. I guess it was an old Oldsmobile or something like that. We barely pulled out of the packing lot when Cheryl stretched out—lying down with her head on my lap and her hands between my thighs gently caressing throughout the forty-five minutes drive. No need to feel guilty or embarrassed or anything. If anything, I was excited, happy and could hardly wait to be home again.

As soon as the door opened, she went to bed. Despite the fact that one of her favorites soap Oprah "All my children" was on when we arrived at my place, she went to bed. I even asked if she would want something to eat. The answer was "no" because she was already in bed.

Lying in bed, I reached out to her. As I was brushing her hair back with my bare hand, she grabbed my hand, kissed it and immediately reached out with the other hand trying to unzip my pant. "I love you." She whispered.

"Are you okay?" I asked. "You look worried. Is there anything you want to talk about?"

"I want you to hold me." She demanded.

Well, I couldn't do that while standing. I dropped the remote control I was holding and joined her in bed. "I love you." I said softly while holding her and gently caressing her body.

"Do you really mean that?' She asked.

"Of course I do. What kind of a question is that?" I responded.

She kissed me and again. "How many women have you made love to so far?" She asked.

"I don't know. I started dating at age 18 or 19. I don't know how many women I've went to bed with since then." I immediately turned the question around. "What about you?"

"Since I've being married or before?"

"Altogether."

"About twenty five, maybe more, it's hard to remember." She said.

"You've been a busy girl." I joked with a smile.

She resumed kissing again from the neck area and gently made her way down to my nipple and below. She then whispered "I don't want to continue like that anymore. I love you and would like to remain with you only."

"Why?" I asked.

"You are very satisfying and very…" She stopped, and then raised her head and looking into my eyes, she said, "You know I love you. You always make me happy and that's one thing I've been looking for a long time." Hands straying and gently caressing, she went below, covered her head and sunk inside the quilted blanket.

I reached out to feel her head. Gently rubbing both hands through her hair, I tried to say something but couldn't get the word out. It got caught in the ecstasy and the excitement of the moment. I felt moisturized and we went on and on.

It was around 6:30pm when I decided to take her home. It just started to rain. The evening was cold and soggy and visibility was very poor. She looked more worried and reluctant. At first, I thought it must be the weather. But whatever it was kind of magnified the tiredness apparent on her face. I had no idea what was bothering her. However, it seemed she needed some kind of assurance and comfort.

"What is wrong with you? If you really love me like you've said so many times, you will tell me the truth." I insisted.

"I've always loved you." She said "but I don't think you love me as much as I love you."

"How do you mean?" I asked.

"Each time I find someone I really like…" She started crying. "I…I thought you…I don't know why you can…" Groping and gasping, she was shaking uncontrollably.

Driving with one hand, while holding her very close with the other hand, I urged her to please talk to me.

With the howling wind, the rain, and the engine noise, she started in a voice that seemed barely adequate. "How can you do that to your own girl friend?" She asked.

"What did I do?" I wanted to know.

"How dare you tell Eileen about our affairs?"

"What are you talking about?

"You know damn well what I'm talking about. Everything you told Eileen…She called me last night and told me all about it including how you are going to abandon our love and the passion we both share. She also told me about some of the things you are planning on…How dare you?"

I felt betrayed. The connection I've been trying to prevent is made. Eileen had managed to sneak into Cheryl's life, thereby, developed an unholy alliance. "Do you really believe that I said anything to Eileen about you?" I asked.

"Oh yes! You bet I do." She said determinedly.

I knew beyond the shadow of doubt that the connection was definitely made. The thing that had been nagging at the back of my mind is now a reality. "How long has the two of you been cooking up lies about me? How much of Eileen have I been dealing with lately through you?" I demanded to know and I was angry.

"Now you think Eileen is lying? Why would she lie about something as confidential as this?"

"Do you remember Coleen Bamford? Eileen's sister? Do you remember my relationship with her before I met you?"

"Don't use that as an excuse." She shouted. "Eileen told me she could care less about that."

"I never knew you could be so naive." I snapped. "What do you need to see the hidden interest of Eileen in all of these, a degree in psychoanalysis?" I shook my head. "I never knew you could be easily manipulated, thereby; turn against the person you said you love! Something is wrong somewhere. There is more to all of these than meet the eyes." Eyebrow rose questioningly, I asked, "You mean to tell me that with all these on your mind, you agreed to make love? How absurd? You are such a…"

"Go ahead. Say it. You want to call me a slut?" She yelled.

"Don't put words in my mouth." I scolded. "I was going to say you are such a complex individual."

"Yeah right!" She said sarcastically.

I pulled up in front of her house; she got out of the car very angry and slammed the door so hard I was surprised she didn't break the door. She went into her house with tears in her eyes.

7

When we met the following day, Cheryl said "hi" and nothing more for a few minutes. Still irritated and offended by her unexpected reaction the night before, I was a little reluctant and withdrawn. She reached out into her pocket and gave me a tape by Jan Adden entitled "Insensitive." She demanded I listen to it either right away or as soon as possible.

"I hope you are not implying anything!" was the only words out of my mouth. By now I was ready to call it quit. My mind became filled with anger and resentment not at anybody in particular but the past including everything and everybody connected to it. I couldn't blame Cheryl for any of these. Instead, I turned inward and started to self assess myself.

In my mind I kept saying: "its ok, this is not your fault...I wouldn't have been in this situation if not..."

On the other hand, I couldn't help but questioning myself "how did I get into this lustful desire with Cheryl? How did I get on this sinful path in search of true love?" The answer did not come.

I thought I could never be swindled. Not after all I've been through. It's not like I refused to listen to the voice of reason. If any, I couldn't hear it. It's been a long time and I was too captivated with one thing on my mind. Cheryl knew what that one thing was. According to her, she too was looking for the same thing. She wanted to be loved and experience the physical excitement that comes with being loved.

At first, she was too vague about her marital status. When I finally realized she's married (which was over nine weeks into this relationship), to say that I was disappointed was an understatement. I was crushed. We were too deeply involved emotionally. We had spent a lot of private and passionate moments together. What can I do? It was too late to back off easily. She had won my heart and I was under the illusion that she might be the one for me. I should have known but I didn't. When I confronted her for the truth with regard to her marriage, she became cool, aloof, and somewhat afraid. She promised never to let go. The more I tried, the harder it gets.

A few days after, as I was bringing her back to her home after a long day at my place, she was hysterical and started to cry and shaking again. She scared the day-light out of me. I promised never to see her anymore but I came back the follow-ing day due to the fear of the unknown such as a possible pregnancy etc. Also, she had said so many times she would never go quietly. I wanted to know what she meant by that.

Notwithstanding, the affairs was coming to an end and she knew that nothing was going to stop me. I wasn't interested in quick and easy seizure but a lasting relationship. She knew we were approaching the beginning of the end of what-ever it was between us.

I wasn't interested in intimacy as much anymore. Her attitude changed even though she did not stop calling or stop coming to my place.

When I finally received a copy of the affidavit and read the charges against me which was based in large part on what she said, I remembered her promises of never to go quietly.

Deeply immersed in the reading of the affidavit, I flipped over to a new page. As I was about to start reading, I heard the voice of Correctional Officer Dan Daquila over the intercom saying to every inmate in the mod: "stand in front of your cell door if you don't want to miss your meal time, otherwise, you will be locked up in your cell you fucking assholes."

Coming out of my cell, an inmate by the name Kemah Tolston called "Hey Doc.! You made the bail?"
"I haven't talk to my friend yet." I responded.
"Call him!" He exclaimed.
"I'm going to do that during our rec. time after lunch." I said sluggishly.
"I understand your X is the one trying to help put the bail money together?" One of the new inmates asked. "Damn! I don't get it…If you are such a bad motherfucker, one thing your X would rather have is to see your ass in jail perma-nently. Man! You must be good that all these women are dying to see you back

out there." He shook his head as he whispered to the inmate standing next to him "that motherfucking nigger is getting out, man!"

"Watch your mouth. He doesn't like to be called that stupid name." His inmate friend said to him.

"What did you say just now, don't you ever call me that again—never! Understand?" I snapped.

"Hey Doc.!" Kemah yelled. "He was just kidding with you. You know he is new around here. We all know you don't like that word." With a shift in his voice he asked, "What's the matter? You are feeling down?"

Kemah, a life liner, was about to begin doing time for assault with deadly weapon and attempted robbery. He went to jail for the first time at age 21 years for dealing drugs and was also involved in abusing drugs—heroine, cocaine, etc. He came home one morning about 6:00am hallucinating and started to abuse his girl friend. That morning, as he latter describes it, he looked like a monster and his girl friend became extremely petrified and unable to sleep next to him. She waited until he was asleep, called the Police and just like that Kemah was arrested. The girl friend also was arrested for being a public nuisance.

While awaiting sentencing on the attempted robbery and assault charges, Kemah decided to find a positive way to cope with the boring and demeaning jail life. As a porter, Kemah was a very hardworking person. As a fellow "sons of a bitch" and a life liner, he often times like to tease and trick people, make them laugh or somehow keep their minds occupied to avoid feeling depressed and forgotten by society.

As he was talking to me, I could hear another inmate saying to someone "that motherfucker is likely to get 8 years in this joint for assault with deadly weapon? Holy-shit!"

"Shut the fuck up." The inmate he was talking to yelled back. "You will do time for your crime, so what is the fucking difference here?"

Focusing on Kemah, I asked "do you think dealing drug and the abusing of it worth your time in jail?"

"Not one second of my time." He said.

"What do people get from using drugs? They get so elevated in their minds; they think they are on top of the world. When they come back down, they discover their systems are all messed up; their minds are not processing information like it should. They become agitated, irrational, and completely out of focus and their bodies are crying for more. Instead of feeling better, now they are worse off. Money is gone and friends are not any closer. Each time their minds open up slightly for them to think realistically, they become so depressed and angry at their hopeless condition. What happens next? They go back into the drug circle again. Before they realize what's going on, they are either in trouble with the law or become so sick they can hardly leave the house. Do you think this is fair?" I asked.

Holding my hands, Kemah said "Doc. You don't belong here. Get the bail money and get the hell out of this place. You are a big brother. Will you promise to stay in touch with me?" He raised his eyebrow questioningly.

"Of course!" I responded.

"I'm going to need the help of people like you. All I can do now is exercise daily just trying to put myself together mind and body. I would want you to please stay in touch with me if you don't mind."

The sound of his voice was quickly drowned in the yelling and screaming of people saying that the government or the police violated their rights.

"This State is all fucked up, man. Rhode Island is the only State that just like to violate your right—time and again." One inmate yelled.

"Many people who are not supposed to be in this 'joint' are here because the system is all fucked up, and the hassle they make you go through is unbelievable." Another inmate said.

"Have you ever thought this could be a perfect case of racism and extreme prejudice?" One inmate asked me when we were going back to our cells. "This white girl friend of yours, have you ever thought she could be part of the plot against you? Look at it this way, if she is not a racist or at least somewhat prejudice—it could be that some racist group sent her. Have you ever thought about that?"

"It can't be…but thanks for the thought." I said

"Why are you so sure?" He asked.

"I've been in business long enough to know." I said confidently. "I am not unaware of the fact that there are some mediocre minds out there who may feel threatened by your efforts." I smiled. "They don't know how to compete anymore. They are very good at destroying things. These angels of death are not too difficult to spot. Believe me, I know these people when I see them and I don't think Cheryl could be part of them in any way shape or form."

"You think you do!" He exclaimed in a high baritone like voice. "You are just like my uncle, always trying to intellectualize everything. Forget about that college bullshit." He raised his voice angrily. "What is it going to take you guys to see that there are some bitches who are sent to give you good fuck in order to screw up your life? Why are black people so blind, man?" With a shift in his voice and eyebrow raised, he went on "I bet when you come out of this joint, you are going to see that bitch and those motherfuckers who arrested you are all in the same camp. You mark my words." He shook his finger. "This is the same game white people have played for so many years. Yet, them nigger brothers don't get it, man. Excuse my language." He said. "I've made a promise not to use that word anymore—but do you understand what I'm trying to tell you?"

"Loud and clear." I responded.

"I don't mean to be rude, but you really have to understand my point." He said. "This is a new age and I don't mean that in a religious sense. We don't believe things simply because Charlie says it's okay to believe it. To heck with Charlie! It used to be that a Brother will come to you and say 'Charlie told me you ain't Accountant. Charlie said you ain't good Attorney, or Charlie said you don't know what you are talking about.' The new attitude now is 'fuck Charlie.' The reason is because we are not going to allow any white individual to put down the best in the African American communities anymore." Irked and annoyed, he went on "when they really want to make their hate filled stories believable, they go in your distance past to open a different kind of warm. Is there anybody who doesn't have some dirty laundries in their pasts? They know how to cover their own just to expose that of Black people. Gosh, I'm so angry." He looked straight into my eyes and said "how many times have you seen a Black person accorded the fucking status of expert in anything by any of the fucking major television stations? How many times have you seen something positive about Africa? Everything we know is all about sickness, hunger, war and the effect of war. What about progress, no matter how tiny?"

Systematic research about race relation will no doubt reveal a lot but in the end the truth about why some are still struggling while others are enjoying abundant success lies in the angry expressions of the oppressed, or hunches of those who are blessed with innate and peculiar ability of being able to read between the lines.

8

I could have sworn Cheryl was real and true. Except for being too emotional and for occasional display of signs and symptoms of a mild hysteria not otherwise classified, nothing to suggest she could be part of an elaborate scheme designed by some privileged government employees.

Whined like a thwarted child, her lips were the only things moving as she sat in the conference room of my newly opened Providence office. She was saying something to a police officer on Friday February 27, 1998. I thought I knew her, but I was stunned and thunderstruck at seeing her true color.

I wouldn't have had the chance to see the other side of Cheryl if not for the actions of Tracey Camara a.k.a. Tracey Walsh.

Tracey, an extremely strange, irrational and very selfish individual with little or no regard whatsoever for the right of others. She's very obsessed with always having her way and could care less whom she stepped over. She first came to the Fall River office on one of those few sweltering days in September. A good number of people had come off the street about the same time. Her application did not attract attention whatsoever and there was no reason for me to call her for interview. Somehow, she was later hired by Eileen as a homemaker, and no one in the office knew until two weeks later when she came to submit her time slips.

Why would Eileen ignore every rule to hire someone with very little experience in healthcare? She's very rude, arrogant, manipulative, loud mouth and very difficult to get along with. Without exaggerating the fact, Tracey is the kind of person (to use the words of Frederick Douglas) "artful enough to descend to the lowest trickery and obdurate enough to be insensitive to the voice of reproaching conscience." It just didn't matter how the ultimate goal is achieved. As far as she's concerned the ends justify the means.

At first, Cheryl and Tracey couldn't get along. Remember Cheryl and Eileen? We are back in the same old hoax and carefully planned swindle of all swindles. Guarded by some unknown plan intricately nested web of intent to turn things around, Cheryl became Tracey's very close friend about three days after they actually met face to face.

It was 8:45 am on Friday February 27, 1998 when I walked into my office. With a cup of tea in my hand, I sprung over to the window. As soon as I rose up the window blind, my face was flooded with the sunlight as I stood there breathing in the morning air while enjoying my tea. Within seconds, I remembered I needed to make some copies before my Secretary comes in.

I came out of my office and walked toward the copy machine which was situated farther left of the front desk and across from Cheryl's office. I had just turned on the copier, my back toward the front desk, and about to make my first copy when I heard Tracey Camara saying "here he is."

I turned around and there she was at the front desk with two police officers. Tracey raised her voice and said "I want my money and I want it now."

Almost immediately, the two police officers said "we are only here to maintain the peace. Are you going to give her the money?"

Before I could answer the police officers, Cheryl walked by and went straight to her office and the same with my Secretary, Oak Chimm. Neither of them said anything. Cheryl did not act like someone aware of what was going on.

Why would Tracey come yelling and screaming in the company of two police officers asking for a pay check first thing on Friday morning? She's been working for me for over two months. Firstly, we don't release pay checks until after 12 noon. Secondly, before you can be paid you have to turn in your time slips and your weekly report. She is aware of all these.

"Could you ask her to give me her time slips and her report to justify whatever money she's asking for." I said to the two police officers.
They asked her but she refused.
One of the two officers asked me "are you going to pay her the money?"
I said "No. Not until I see her time slips and her weekly report."

The other officer made a phone call and two more police officers joined the previous two. When the two new officers walked in, Tracey's story changed. She was now screaming sexual harassment and sexual abuse. Cheryl Arruda, her friend and my office manager came out of her office. At seeing the four police officers, she started crying and shaking. One of the officers took her to our glass wall conference room. The police officer talked to Cheryl behind closed door for about 10 minutes. After that Cheryl came to her office and was immediately packing everything into a large trash bag she brought. Why would she bring such a large trash bag for something that could have fit into a packable? When I saw something that look like a bunch of manilla files going inside of the trash bag, I asked the police officer to let me examine the bag. The police officer refused.

"We have to remove everybody from here because of the alleged sexual harassment." One of the police officers said.

Before I could say anything, they asked everybody including my Secretary—Oak Chimm and two other employees who sat quietly while all these were going on to leave right away.

Mystified and upset, I sat in my office trying to rationalize the drama that just took place. How the demands for paycheck evolved into an alleged sexual harassment and the police's decision to remove all my employees from my office. It just didn't make sense.

Another bizarre twist to the whole story was the fact that Gerard Danna of the Attorney General's office called two investigative reporters from Channel 10 on that same Friday to follow up on the alleged sexual harassment story. If anything, is that the proper way to investigate something this serious? More importantly, who called the AG's office? Could it be that they were in on the whole thing right from the beginning? Anyway, Jim Taricani and Dyana Koelsh of Channel 10 went to Cheryl's house and from there to Tracey and finally to Denise MaClin who I fired first week in February for wrongdoing. The fact that all of these unexpected events happened the same Friday raised many unanswered questions.

Despite all that took place in the morning, Cheryl and Oak Chimm came back around 1:00 p.m. to pick up their final paychecks.

I thought I was just a quiet and unknown healthcare Administrator trying to do my best against all odds. Instantly, one event turned my world upside down.

Everything got thrown into the hands of some local investigative reporters interested in sensationalizing lies and innuendoes.

On Monday March 2, 1998 at about 9:00 am a telephone call came in from Jim and Dyana. "We are doing a story on healthcare and would like to get your professional opinion" was their request.

"Why me?" I asked.

"Why not you?" was the reply. "You have been in healthcare for so many years. We just need your professional opinion."

"Could you give me an idea of what you are coming to talk about?" I demanded.

"It's simple. You don't have to worry about it." Jim said.

I agreed to meet with them the following day at 9 am. I came prepared thinking that the interview might bring something positive. I did not know that they were aware of what took place at my office on Friday February 27.

Except for the initial greetings, nothing friendly. It was one attack after another and when Jim brought up the sexual harassment story, he said, "we are going to feature your story." "What do you think would happen when your clients sees this on the TV?" He asked. This is not an empty threat. Jim knew that there are great deals of people who like to be fed on a steady diet of bad news even if it is a total fabrication.

Right away, I was overwhelmed with fear. To say that I lost my mind was an understatement. I became seriously discouraged. My blood pressure must have gone way up. For the first time in my life, I felt abandoned and lonely. Frantically, I went looking for someone to talk to. Somehow, I found the love of God in John Duffy. John is a lawyer by training but a Public Relation Officer by profession. He came to my office, talked for a while and demanded we go out for a cup of coffee. For hours, John was with me and refused to leave until he was certain beyond the shadow of doubt that I was all right and that I would not do something stupid. We left the office building almost at the same time and he gave me his home telephone number just in case.

Around 7:30 pm, State Trooper Elwood called. "Are you okay?" He asked. He kept me on the telephone and did his best to be sure everything was fine. I guess you could call it "touched by Angels." Both John and Officer Elwood went beyond the call of duty. They decided to be co-workers with God. I will never forget it.

You can search the entire dictionary and you will not find one word to describe the new kind of racism unfolding in this real life scenario. How the eruption of a new prejudice and realignment of bigotry found another carefully constructed vehicle at the Rhode Island Attorney General's office. Those who are suppose to protect the people regardless of the color of their skin are actually busy devising tactical lynching mechanism from which to shatter dreams, demoralize and make criminals out of minorities who dare to stick their necks out. They were on a very serious mission to destroy.

I came to the office very early in the morning on Thursday March 5, 1998. I call the police before 9am to report some missing files and important papers. The police had barely walked into my office when the telephone rang. I picked it up at the front desk and it was Gerard Danna of the Attorney General's office. He asked if I would be able to bring the information they had previously requested from me.

"Sure" was my immediate reply. "There are some files missing and I called the police office this morning to report those missing files and other information taken by Cheryl Arruda."

"Is the police there now?" Gerard asked.

"Yes." I responded.

"May I talk to him?" He demanded.

Although it looked somewhat strange to me but I did not object. I gave the telephone to the police officer and said, "The AG's office would like to talk to you."

After a brief conversation, the police officer said to me "I am not going to write any report with regard to your missing records but if you still have further concerns, feel free to call us back." This man gave me the cold shoulder in spite of his oath "to protect and to serve."

"What did that guy from the AG's office tell you?" I asked.

"Nothing. Like I said, if you still have further concerns, feel free to call us back." The police officer said again as he walked out the door.

If you think racism, prejudice, and cultural biases are gone, think again. There are those who believe that the Ku Klux Klan are too loud; the skinheads and the

Aryan nations are too easy to detect. These new enemies of mankind would rather use their positions to create psychological warfare powerful than nuclear energy. In the words of Alvin Toffler author of the Third Wave, "Humanity faces a quantum leap forward. It faces the deepest social upheaval and creative restructuring of all time."

9

In attempting an unprecedented large scale of synthesized lies and hate, these agents of destruction went down to the lowest of the low in their effort to brainwash, misinform, and insult the intelligence of the people.

On April 6 one of the guards reminded me of the court appearance coming up the following day.

From that moment on, I became a little anxious. I couldn't sleep. The night seemed very long I must have woke up about four or five times. Although I had a feeling, however, nothing to indicate that this was my last night in prison. The end of my 28 days of incarceration.

It was 7:00 am when a female correctional officer came knocking "'14 bottom', get up, you are going to court this morning." For some seconds she stood staring at me perhaps thinking if I would get up or go back to sleep.
I got up and was ready within minutes.
My cellmate whispered "good luck, man."
"Don't tell me you knew what this is all about."
"It must be your bail hearing." He said softly. "I don't think you are coming back here. I heard one of guys who went to court yesterday saying something about your bail. I think they came up with the money to get you out."

As I pushed the door open, I realized this might be my first day of freedom in 28 days. I turned around and said to my cellmate "Hey kid! I wish you luck too." There were about four of us from the same mod. We were asked to go to the cafeteria where we joined with over 100 inmates going to court that same morning. I glanced slyly at the back breaking bed and demeaning environment I was about to leave behind for good. My eyes met the officer's eyes and she smiled. It was beginning to feel like freedom.

About five minutes after we walked into the courthouse, I heard my name called, and was immediately whisked before the judge. From the moment I saw the bail bondsman signing a paper, I knew I wasn't going back to the ACI. I looked over my shoulder and saw my friend Rev P.F. sitting there with a big smile on his face. I couldn't help returning it with another big smile. I turned around and the judge asked me to sign. After that, the sheriff to my right grabbed his keys and removed the shackle. The total effect struck me like a big wave. I wanted to jump and shout for joy but that seemed totally awkward. However, I looked up and whispered "thank you."

I walked out of the courthouse like some kind of a political hero with the bail bondsman on one side and my friend on the other.

The memory of that demeaning arrest and series of mind numbing cruelty that followed resurfaced again for about a week. A few days later, I finally summoned enough courage to open my mails. In this mountain of junk mails and some business mails was my bank statement. Despite the fact that I pulled the statement aside, I did not open it until a couple of days later. In the statement was a payroll check with my name signed to it allegedly by the payee. I called the payroll processing company only to discover that a payroll was processed when I was at the ACI.

Cheryl, my so called girl friend and also office manager, who left my company on February 27 called "Paychex" which was the payroll-processing center for my company and asked them to process payroll for alleged work done during the period ending March 14, 1998. According to Cheryl, the work was done by the following people: Cheryl Arruda, Tracey Camara, Denise MaClin, Oak Chimm, Leann Lynn, and Keith Santere. You have to remember that the Providence police officers that came to my office on 2/27/98 removed all my employees and I was arrested on 3/9/98 and the business closed down immediately. Not only that, Denise MaClin was fired the first week in February, Tracey Camara quit on 2/25/98. Why are these people showing up on my company's payroll now? Who was behind the processing of these unauthorized pay checks?

Cheryl called the payroll processing company and asked them to process payroll without permission and for work that was never performed. Checks dated 3/24/98 along with payroll information were sent on 3/23/98 to the home address of Cheryl Arruda and my signature forged on each check. Two checks went through the bank—Cheryl and Tracey's. Cheryl's check was paid and Tracey's $836.51 returned.

My bank statement revealed a payroll check number 1258 dated 3/24/98 in the amount of $739.42 made payable to Cheryl Arruda. The check was paid on 4/16/98. The gross total of payroll processed for these people was $4,016.00 with a net of $3,253.21.

I've always been fascinated by the parallel between stupidity, hate, and prejudice. Even though we can only remember the past and not the future, the ability to think about the consequences of our actions before it occurs provide us the only window to see the future. To ignore this kind of consequential reasoning would eventually lead to breaking of the law.

To begin with, what these people (Cheryl, Tracey and Denise) said explicitly in addition to what was attributed to them implicitly was what prompted my arrest for something or some things I knew nothing about. Could it be that their sense of reasoning took a vacation the moment I was arrested or somebody bragged that they might put me behind bars for a long time? Whatever or whomever was responsible for their conspiracy to commit crime of this magnitude must have forgotten that "The Most High rules in the kingdom of men."

This criminal act by some of the key players in the conspiracy against me prompted my lawyer to move for a motion to dismiss the case. Without hesitation, the motion was granted.

10

To accomplish the monumental task of trying to build a business requires a focus journey through the pitfalls and triumphs of its enduring lonely road of determination. At times we are so caught up in the process of building and fail to imagine that those who are paid to guide us can actually be more interested in our downfall, is unthinkable. Ironically, they are the people who believe that the world is divided into two separate and distinct camps. One is the camp of the suspicious and the other, the camp of the believed. Even if those in the camp of the suspicious are doing all the right things, yet, they will have more man-made cloud hanging over their heads, more questions to answer, more rivers to cross and a lot of mountains to climb. On the other hand, if those in the camp of the believed are breaking every law on the book and doing all the wrong things, as long as they can call whatever mistakes there are partly oversight and partly unaware, the answer will always be "I believe you."

It is very tragic to see that in this age of great advancement in technology, medicine, business and politics, the color of your skin still determine how successful you are.

The same old plan of every hate group carefully developed to break down structure, meaning, and purpose for living is now responsible for the creative approach of the new regiment. Their minds are bent on trying to legislate or scare minorities out of business hoping that in the end, they will self-destruct.

In Rhode Island, there are more than fifty home care agencies and only four owned by minorities at the time of this unfortunate occurrence back in 1998. Out of these four, three were featured in the television special presented by Jim Taricani and his partner Dyana. The only one not featured was fiercely attacked quietly. Is it by mere coincidence that they were all forced out of business within three months?

I was thrown in jail all because of "he said, she said" and the demented, deranged mind and bigot in charge of the case was not interested in finding out the truth. With his preconceived stereotypical expectations of minorities in his

47

twisted mind, he set himself on a mission to destroy and make criminals out of honest people who are struggling to make their dreams a reality.

However, a date was set for my pre-arraignment. About two days to the pre-arraignment conference, a friend called and gave me a name. He said, "You might want to take a look at this guy's case before you go to court." I was too discouraged to do anything right away until the same name along with two more separate cases came up in a discussion with another friend shortly thereafter.

The name revealed case number P2/97–2926A. I immediately went to the superior court and made a copy of the case. I couldn't believe what I was reading. This affidavit written and signed by Gerard Danna (the guy who initiated my arrest) not only revealed more than I was prepared to know, it made me angry to no end.

The following are excerpts from the two affidavits. Company B is my company. Both affidavits are in the public domain. What that means is you should be able to obtain a copy if you so desire.

Company A—Owned by a Caucasian	Company B—Owned by a African-American
On May 27, 1997, Gerard Dana received a call pertaining to company A. The caller alleged that company A "did bill the State of Rhode Island Medicaid program for services which were not rendered." The EDS bills were reviewed for the period 3/1/1997—5/29/1997 and they reflected that company A billed the State of Rhode Island for $941.16 for the period 3/1/1997—3/31/1997 and $1,104.84 for the period 4/1/1997—4/30/1997. According to Gerard Dana's report, the State of Rhode Island paid those invoices.	On November 14, 1997, Gerard Dana received a call pertaining to company B. The caller alleged that company B "was billing the Medicaid program of Rhode Island for home health services that were not provided…" As reported by Gerard Dana, he reviewed the EDS computer billing records and it revealed that company B was paid for the period 10/1/1997—10/12/1997 in the amount of $350.08. Gerard Dana also reported that another payment for the period 10/13/1997—10/31/1997 in the amount of $175.04 was made to company B.

Company A—Owned by a Caucasian	Company B—Owned by a African-American
What did Gerard Dana do? How did he handle these two cases?	
Gerard Dana interviewed all the parties concerned including the owner of company A (a Caucasian) behind close door. However, Gerard Dana turned around and charged the home health aide (an employee of company A) a Hispanic male with a crime. The home health aide was brought to court on six (6) counts of criminal charges. He was convicted on two and four were dismissed.	As for company B, Gerard Dana called Jim Taricani of the television station Channel 10. The home health aide (a Caucasian girl) was interviewed as well as many employees. However, Gerard Dana turned around, arrested and charged the owner of company B (an African American) with a crime. Gerard Dana and his gang of racist television reporters were preparing a 92 count of criminal charges when their plan fell apart.

What happen to the President and Owner of company A? Nothing whatsoever. Was he ever arrested publicly or otherwise for the crime he committed? Never. Did he get away with crime because of the color of his skin? No doubt about that.

Is it by accident that the result of the 1998 Rhode Island Race Relations study for the National Conference for Community and Justice came while all these were unfolding? Perhaps not. The study revealed how polarized and indifference to each other's problems the people of the smallest state in the union are. "We don't really know each other very well," Anthony Maione the executive director of the local NCCJ said. As reported, "The study confirms the widely held impression that Rhode Island is a segregated state."

Most Rhode Islanders do have genuine love for the human family regardless of the color of your skin. "People in general believe everyone should have an equal opportunity." The problem lies with some demented members of the privileged group who will not accept and love people for who they are. They just want to make life difficult for those who are sincerely struggling and trying to genuinely earn their rightful place in society.

The survey asked why blacks and Hispanics can't get ahead. I think they should ask Gerard Dana and those who like to arrest minorities over "he said, she said" and protect the real criminals because of the color of their skin.

11

What about some members of the media? The people we've come to trust. We take their words as the ultimate truth without the slightest effort to check its validity. They tell us they only report the news and not create them. If that was true, the world would be a better place. I never thought that some of them could be part of the problem and not the solution.

These people who can make rational behavior look irrational (depending on their reporting choice) and vice versa all within few minutes knows perfectly well how to capitalize on our gullible trust of the tube. If the television says it is true, it must be, because it couldn't be otherwise. In essence, they know how lethal misinformation can be and they are not unaware of the fact that from the moment they become a reporter or an anchor person, they are in a way license to kill or save lives depending on which way the pendulum swings.

They know how to manipulate symbols, words, and sentences. They don't have to necessarily subscribe to the basic premise of inductive and deductive reasoning. They may present themselves as investigative reporters; investigative to some of these people is a subjective term. They are not interested in the truth just something to feed on the people's hunger for bad news.

These people who are well aware of the damaging effect of half-truth, took whatever was given to them and blew it completely out of proportion. They are not unaware of the fact that there are some people who will not hesitate to make up stories most especially if they know that the Attorney General's office is looking into something about you.

In the story they did about me was a man they said is a Medical Doctor currently doing 15 years in a federal prison for similar offence. His face was blocked out and his name was never revealed. They stated that the picture and the story of the man were from the FBI file. Couple of months later, I called Jim Taricani for the man's name and the nature of his crime just to read about it. If this man was arrested, tried and convicted, why would anybody want to protect his identity only to splash the identity of someone who in the eyes of the law is "innocent until proven guilty?"

If that man committed the crime in his own office as reported by Jim Taricani, why did he wear a black leather glove in an environment that didn't look like a medical practitioner's office? Jim Taricani did not reveal this man's name or the nature of his crime and according to Jim he did not know the man's name or anything about him.

As it turned out, the man wasn't even a medical doctor and his so called offence (if ever there was one) wasn't even healthcare related. Could it be that the man was just an actor! Possibly! His story was included in an attempt to deceive the public, thereby, legitimize lies and total fabrications.

12

I had a dream. And my dream was to one day become my own boss just like many people has done not only in the US but all over the world and many continue to do. What a simple dream! I knew that making it a reality wasn't going to be easy. I knew I might somehow have to swallow my pride to take insult and rejection courageously all in the effort to make my dream a reality. I knew I might have to bend backward just to accommodate some people I could have otherwise avoided. I knew I would have to endure or sacrifice a lot. Little did I know it might someday place me "between justice and injustice, between the forces of light and the forces of darkness?"

I was not naïve to think there is a single society where prejudice is non-existent. But when you take a careful look at the role of the United States in the world, you can't but wonder. A nation rightly ordained to become a save haven for "the tired, the poor, and the hurdle masses" of the world. United States of America is the microcosm of the planet earth. It does not have a prevailing culture or tradition, hence, the lack of cultural or traditional rulers such as kings, queens, chiefs or emperors. It cannot pride itself as the largest democracy but the most democratic nation. The only country under heaven capable of standing against apartheid, hunger and starvation, tyranny, intent to rig election, tribal intolerance, and genocide all around the world. The only nation jointly established by Europeans, Africans, Latinos, Asians, Orientals, Arabs, Jews, and Indians—Native Americans and those from the land of Mahatma K. Gandhi.

I was so confident that if anything, this is a place where dreams can come true. I knew there would be many rough and crooked places along the way; I knew there would be some winding and meandering road to travel. Many of successful men and women all over the world made it amid a rich legacy of trials, tribulations, and struggle. Among others, some things they all have in common include unrelenting faith in their dreams and the willingness to swim against the tide.

I knew it wasn't going to be easy: there will be many rivers to cross, sacrifices to be made and a lot to endure.

However, I never knew there were some people, some deranged, conniving, and sick minds, laying in ambush even in the land of the free and the home of the brave. I never knew there is a wildfire revival of racial war and intensifying cultural biases so neatly embellished in the execution of policies both government and corporate.

Organized conspiracy against group or race is undeniably real. Although, it is rooted in the vitriolic act of those greedy and demented minds of the racist few. However, the extraordinary quiet absorption of evil, implicit in misinterpretation and selfish analysis of data by some biased, narrow-minded members of the privileged group in conjunction with the approval of the scientific community remains in large part to be blamed for the never ending circle of oppression.

The Need of an individual to "strive to realize his life by losing and finding himself in something greater than himself" cannot be over emphasized. The desire to practice until perfection is reached; study until full understanding is attained; endure until victory is won; and love until hate is defeated, though unnatural to the "constitution of human nature" are necessary ingredients to human living.

I am not the type of individual who like to blame others for my own shortcomings. Projecting blame will do nothing but paralyze the mind, destroy will power, thereby, intensify hate and anger.

I've never said I was too important to stand in the cold and wait for public transportation to take me to my destination; too educated to sleep on mattress if it become necessary to sell my bed to raise money; too weak to eat once a day; too arrogant to take insulting words; or too skilled to do Newspaper delivery. I am much too intelligent to seek immediate outlet that may result in the destruction of my name. I love myself too much to allow that to happen. No single individual can achieve his or her full potential without some degree of self-love. This is what most people will not hesitate to call pride. Without this kind of pride, there can be no sense of shame and guilt. Pride will help you realize that there is more to a good name than a mere recognition. A good name is better than diamond and gold. Beauty and the willingness to take love to a higher level may captivate the mind of man, thereby obscure sense of reasoning, but pride will give you the necessary rude awakening. If pride is applied positively and creatively, you will be able to see what is morally right and dignify. It will also help you find better strategies to achieve your goal.

After I sold my first business, I was determined to still try again. I could have chosen to do something altogether different but the experience gained and connections made over the years prompted me to think about staying in the same line of business. I love myself too much to leave my dream unfulfilled.

Potent redemptive power and self-love are inevitable tools necessary to energize the inner springs of action. Self-love, rightly focused, can help us achieve and maximize our potential through dedication and concentration.

Standing before the avalanche of decisions, I made up my mind to pull myself together and try establishing a business one more time. Part of our basic human right include the right to try and succeed or fail; saddened by failure or elated by success; celebrate the accomplishment of goals or blame your inability to attain goals.

Was I unaware or perhaps underestimated the magnitude of the odds I was up against? Of course not! Did I intentionally underestimate the requirements for success? Nothing could be farther from the truth. What was my motivation? Winning was to me the most important. Winning mattered. With this mindset, I went back to the drawing table.

The first time in business started out as my solution to socioeconomic problems; as a way to put a dent on the overall unemployment picture. The desire to rise above my circumstances, find a solid ground and eventually help someone in need has always been my ultimate goal.

As a service-oriented company, a lot of efforts (sleepless nights and days) went into researching the product to avoid travesty. Strengths and weaknesses of prospective competitors were studied and analyzed. Quality of service was carefully looked into and employees' high rate of turn over was questioned. Family and friends got involved in analyzing all data and information collected. We put all the "ifs", "buts" "wheres" and "whys" into consideration. The outcome of my research was organized and planning concerning implementation began almost immediately.

The company was established, and things were going on well—it was a wonderful experience. Eight years later, I decided to sell the business in order to move into something different but still in healthcare. I was very confident and ready. I was confident in the knowledge gained, and confident in my experience. I knew I was better equipped this time around than when I first started some years earlier. Somehow I felt there were some unfinished parts of my dream and I was not about to give up.

The term "press on" have some very interesting and arresting enduring significance in the quest to make our dreams a reality. In a world that is filled with wonders and surprises even in the midst of what may seem to be unsettling confusion, there is nothing wrong in sticking your neck out in order to realize your dream, most especially when you have a positive look on life.

I believe that the unalienable rights of life, liberty, and the pursuit of happiness including the great beacon light of hope echoed by Thomas Jefferson in the declaration of independence and later made available to the rest of God's children by Abraham Lincoln when he signed the Emancipation Proclamation were indeed meant for all.

I would like to think that the type of jealousy you experience when you go to the book store, pick up a book about Henry Ford, John Rockefeller, and even Bill Gate, and develop the desire to do the same or even better should be seen as dream driven inspiration to be encouraged.

I thought we are living in a society where you can encourage your children to aim high, go for the gold and never limit themselves. That the high school kid working part-time or full-time in the mail room of a U.S. corporation should be encouraged to dream of becoming a department head or a vice president someday.

I strongly believe that all these are possible most especially in the land of the free and the home of the brave. However, one thing I found difficult to believe is that some people are allowed to determine who should or should not succeed in life. To force four minority business owners out of business without wrongdoing constitute a sin against humanity. To even wrap that in some kind of judgment blinding, and baseless accusations with the help of some prejudice television reporters without proper investigation constitute an act of man's inhumanity to man. The applauding silence and indifference of the general public makes me wonder if most people believe that all men are created equal or they just like it because it makes good reading in the constitution. "Our generation," in the words of Dr. King, "will have to repent not only for the words and acts of the children of darkness, but also for the fears and apathy of the children of light."

The power to make dream a reality operates on the internal gyrations of will. Whether a will is strong enough to transform imagination into visible and useful element can sometime depend on either the presence of positive energy otherwise known as inspiration or the persistent effort of the dreamer to refuse to give up.

However, this second time around, the destroyers were ready. They found a perfect ally in two local TV investigative reporters and all of them were waiting and determined not only to stop the continuation of my dream but also to end it all. Somehow they had forgotten that:

> Though the cause of evil prosper
> Yet 'tis truth alone is strong
> Truth forever on the scaffold
> Wrong forever on the throne
>
> Yet that scaffold sways the future
> And behind the dim unknown
> God is standing in the shadow
> Keeping watch above His own.

13

They armed themselves against me and I didn't know. They used the temptation I fell into against me. Filled with hate they came like a roaring lion. I thought they were merely doing their jobs, I didn't know they were on a mission. They were on a specific mission to destroy dreams all because of the color of my skin.

Why do we have to hate each other so bad? No doubt we have so many differences. There should be little or no argument over the fact that our differences are preordained by God. Even within the same culture, you will find countless differences—political, sociological, ideological, philosophical, cultural and spiritual. However, instead of celebrating our differences, we've somehow allowed them to create a very deep gulf of hatred. Why?

To justify discrimination we turned to labeling and stereotypical belief. To say that some people (because of their ethnic background, national origin, creed and color) are inherently lazy or prone to commit crime is nothing short of a deep and serious psychological disorder. To pursue them endlessly to the point of doing everything possible to stop them from living a descent life is not only unfair, it is very sinful and ungodly.

Above all, to provide an escape route for these agent of destruction constitute crime against humanity. Taking responsibility is expected of any public official (elected or appointed), any individual in position of power and even the general public. Judicial immunity on the other hand is giving to some appointed judges, and civil servants in diverse law enforcement. In a way, some among these law enforcement officials believe they are ordained to terrorize those outside of their narrow definition of the human race while others believe it is a privilege and honor to serve humanity.

This methodically crafted act-of-control bureaucracy called judicial immunity is still one of the remaining shields available for the wicked and the oppressor in these day and age. In the US no single individual is guilty until proven innocent unless you fall into the hands of some of those terrorists in uniform or in the

Attorney General's office or in the media. In this great nation, everybody is presumed innocent until proven guilty. If that is the case, why in the world is judicial immunity necessary to protect those who are responsible for intentionally framing innocent people thereby creating an appearance of a crime? Why is it necessary to shield them from taking responsibility for their actions most especially when it is so obvious that they acted with such a Malicious Intent?

Let us assume for a moment that they are merely acting on probable cause. Are we that naïve to think that the so called probable cause can actually grow out of rumors, hearsay, innuendos or purely out of discontent or jealousy between neighbors, friends, co-workers, or just two complete strangers who simply just do not like each other!

How do you justify the action of a law enforcement officer that was called to the scene of a crime, instead of doing the right thing decided to prosecute an innocent bystander and let the criminal completely off the hook. He is probably thinking "I can do whatever I damn please and even if the true reason for doing what I did is discovered, I'm protected by 'judicial immunity.'"

We would like to think that they are hired and put on public payroll in order to protect our interest (regardless of the color of your skin, sexual orientation, national origin or culture) and also to help us to understand those bureaucratic mumbo jumbos.

We would like to believe that if you are stranded anywhere in the United States you can pick up the phone and call any police station, local or state, for protection without having to worry about whether they would act justly.

Why do we still have these bigots and terrorists on the payroll made available by the taxes of Whites, Blacks, Latino, Jews, Asians, Arabs, Indians and many Americans of goodwill? More importantly, why are we using the taxes collected from "we the people" to protect these racists?

978-0-595-39009-0
0-595-39009-9

www.ingramcontent.com/pod-product-compliance
Lightning Source LLC
Chambersburg PA
CBHW020357290526
45785CB00005B/2334